DEALING WITH
MENTAL DISORDERS

DEALING WITH
ANXIETY DISORDER

By A.W. Buckey

San Diego, CA

© 2020 ReferencePoint Press, Inc.
Printed in the United States

For more information, contact:
ReferencePoint Press, Inc.
PO Box 27779
San Diego, CA 92198
www.ReferencePointPress.com

ALL RIGHTS RESERVED.

No part of this work covered by the copyright hereon may be reproduced or used in any form or by any means—graphic, electronic, or mechanical, including photocopying, recording, taping, web distribution, or information storage retrieval systems—without the written permission of the publisher.

Content Consultant: Carla Marie Manly, PhD

LIBRARY OF CONGRESS CATALOGING-IN-PUBLICATION DATA

Names: Buckey, A. W., author.
Title: Dealing with anxiety disorder / A. W. Buckey.
Description: San Diego : ReferencePoint Press, 2020. | Series: Dealing with mental disorders | Includes bibliographical references and index. | Audience: Grades 10-12.
Identifiers: LCCN 2019034022 (print) | LCCN 2019034023 (eBook) | ISBN 9781682827857 (hardcover) | ISBN 9781682827864 (eBook)
Subjects: LCSH: Anxiety disorders--Juvenile literature. | Anxiety disorders--Treatment--Juvenile literature.
Classification: LCC RC531 .B83 2020 (print) | LCC RC531 (ebook) | DDC 616.85/22--dc23
LC record available at https://lccn.loc.gov/2019034022
LC ebook record available at https://lccn.loc.gov/2019034023

CONTENTS

INTRODUCTION
WHEN WORRY TAKES OVER............... 4

CHAPTER ONE
WHAT ARE ANXIETY DISORDERS? 10

CHAPTER TWO
HOW ARE ANXIETY DISORDERS DIAGNOSED?................................26

CHAPTER THREE
WHAT IS LIFE LIKE WITH ANXIETY DISORDERS? 44

CHAPTER FOUR
HOW ARE ANXIETY DISORDERS TREATED? 54

SOURCE NOTES 70
FOR FURTHER RESEARCH 74
INDEX 76
IMAGE CREDITS............................. 79
ABOUT THE AUTHOR....................... 80

INTRODUCTION

WHEN WORRY TAKES OVER

Lixi is a tenth grader with a full life. Like many high school students, she juggles a lot of responsibilities. Lixi thinks ahead to the weekend. On Friday afternoon, she has to give a multimedia presentation in her World History class. She has plans to go see a movie with friends later that night. On Saturday, she'll compete in the hurdles at the regional track meet. And her dad will expect her to help with some chores before the weekend is over. Lixi has plenty of practice managing a busy schedule. But for the past year, she's found it harder and harder to handle and enjoy her life. Instead of moving through the present, she feels paralyzed by worries about the future.

As Lixi sits down to work on her project, her mind turns to worst-case scenarios. What if she can't finish her research in time? What if she slips up and makes an embarrassing mistake in front of the class? If she messes up, her teacher might decide to fail her. It would be so hard to come back to class after that. She tries to make progress on her work, but her fear of mistakes makes it hard to concentrate. The blinking cursor

Small levels of anxiety are normal. But high levels of anxiety can interfere with daily life and make once-enjoyable activities something to dread.

on her laptop screen makes her feel tense and nervous. If she can't finish her work now, will she ever be able to do it?

Lixi wants to look forward to relaxing with her friends. But lately, the thought of being around people feels overwhelming. She worries that

Anxiety affects people differently. Some people might feel sleepy, and some might have trouble sleeping.

she'll say the wrong thing or even look at people the wrong way. A trip to the movies feels like a social minefield. She imagines her friends getting impatient with her and strangers judging her. Some of her oldest friends have noticed her discomfort, but they're not sure why she's acting differently. They don't know how to help her. Lixi finds herself going out less because spending time with friends creates so much stress.

Lixi used to love running track. She enjoyed the thrill of competition and striving for a personal best. This past year, though, her performance has slipped. She doesn't enjoy competing like she used to. Lixi has trouble going to sleep. She feels tired and drained during the day, but at night she can't seem to turn off her brain and unwind. When she wakes up, she doesn't feel truly rested. Her shoulders ache, even when she hasn't worked out, and she gets headaches easily. It's harder to run her fastest when she feels tired and on edge for so much of the day. And the energizing tension she used to feel before a meet—the kind that spurred her to do her best—has been replaced with dread.

It's normal to have worries and fears. Everyone goes through stressful times. But Lixi's feelings of anxiety and stress never seem to go away. Instead of inspiring her to do her best, her anxiety makes it difficult for her to live her life. She's been feeling this way for months, with no sign of a positive change. Lixi uses her research skills to look up her symptoms online. She realizes that she fits the description of a person with GAD, or generalized anxiety disorder. She talks with her parents about her research. They all decide Lixi should visit her doctor to talk about what she is going through. They know the doctor will have more information for her.

ANXIETY DISORDERS

There are many people with stories like Lixi's. According to the *Diagnostic and Statistical Manual of Mental Disorders, 5th Edition,* GAD is a disorder that causes "excessive anxiety and worry . . . about a number of events or activities."[1] It affects about 3 percent of the US population each year.

> "People with GAD don't know how to stop the worry cycle and feel it is beyond their control."[2]
> – Anxiety and Depression Association of America

People with GAD realize that they worry more than they need to. However, according to the Anxiety and Depression Association of America (ADAA), "People with GAD don't know how to stop the worry cycle and feel it is beyond their control."[2] This cycle of worry, stress, and anxiety has a persistent negative effect on their lives. The National Institute of Health (NIH) states that people with GAD "startle easily, can't relax, and can't concentrate."[3] GAD is one of several anxiety disorders. Some anxiety disorders involve specific stressors, and each disorder has different symptoms and effects. However, anxiety disorders are alike in a few key ways. GAD and other anxiety disorders cause lasting feelings of stress, worry, and fear that make everyday life difficult.

Anxiety disorders are the most common type of mental illness in the United States. They affect almost 20 percent of adults in America each year. Anxiety disorders are caused by a combination of factors, including "genes, stress, and the environment," according to scientist and psychiatrist Daniel Pine.[4] Anxiety disorders can have devastating effects on sufferers' lives. People with anxiety disorders are more likely to be hospitalized for mental illness than other people. They may find themselves limiting their lives due to anxiety, shutting out activities and relationships

> "Anxiety disorders are one of the most treatable mental health problems."[5]
> – Daniel Pine, MD, scientist and psychiatrist

Anxiety disorders are a type of mental disorder. They are the most common mental disorder in the United States, affecting about 20 percent of adults.

in order to avoid their fears. However, according to Dr. Pine, "anxiety disorders are one of the most treatable mental health problems."[5] People with anxiety disorders can manage and relieve their symptoms with the help of therapy, medication, and self-help strategies.

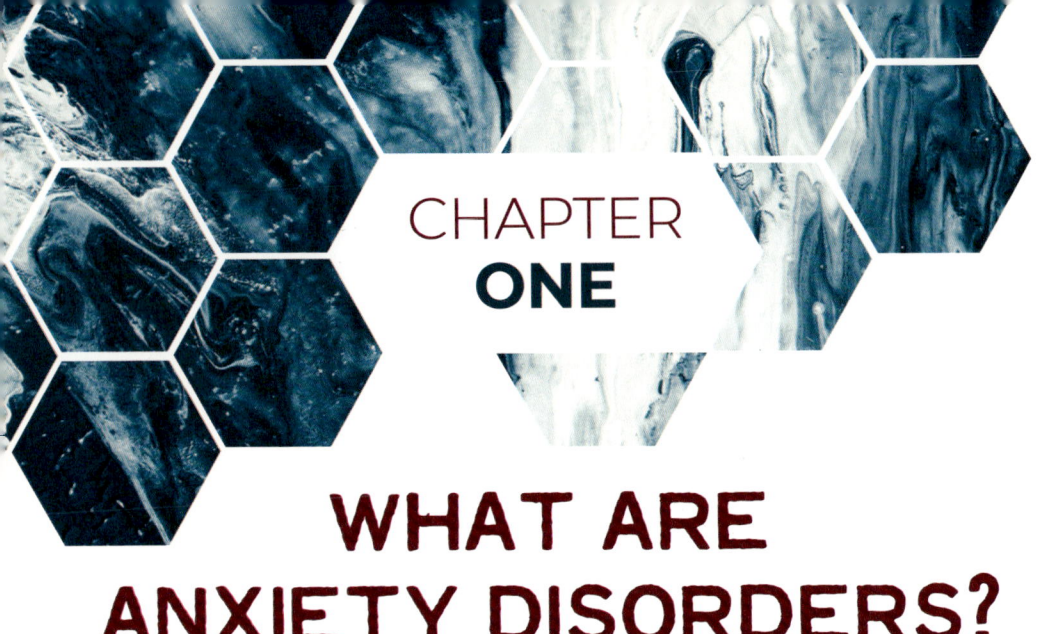

CHAPTER ONE

WHAT ARE ANXIETY DISORDERS?

Anxiety is a universal emotion. Like fear, anxiety is a response to something threatening or unwanted. Anxiety also includes worry, or thoughts and concerns that interrupt peace of mind. What makes anxiety unique is that it persists even when no threat is present, and it is felt in the body as well as the mind. Fear is usually a response to an immediate danger. A person who sees a big snake may feel symptoms of fear, such as mental alertness and physical tension. A person with anxiety about snakebites will feel some of those sensations even when there are no snakes around. They may worry about snakes appearing at unlikely times and places. Anxiety is the negative anticipation of things that may or may not happen in the future.

Anxiety is a physical and mental response. There is no single experience of anxiety, but instead a complex cluster of thoughts and sensations. Anxiety can be felt in the body through symptoms such as fast breathing, sweating, shaking, and an upset stomach. People can experience anxiety very differently. For example, some people with anxiety

Anxiety disorders disrupt a sufferer's life. They affect both the body and the mind.

may feel sleepy and have trouble concentrating, while others may feel unusually tense and unable to sleep. Some may feel too cold when they're anxious, while others may feel overheated. Anxiety also often involves repetitive, concerning thoughts. People who are feeling anxiety may find themselves imagining worst-case scenarios or fixating on a negative outcome for some future event.

Anxiety is not pleasant or fun to experience. But like all emotions, it has useful purposes. Anxiety can help us prepare for important or dangerous situations. The worry and tension it produces can help us concentrate, prepare, and do our best. A slight increase in anxiety can actually optimize performance. This is sometimes called optimal anxiety. Feeling anxious about a big game can motivate us to practice hard and strategize. Anxiety can also be a clue that tells us about our priorities. Having anxiety about an upcoming project can be a sign that it's important to do well. Anxiety is also normal in personal relationships and social situations. It's natural to want to make a good impression on others, and people tend to worry about the well-being of their closest relatives and friends. Moments of anxiety can spur us to action or help us make good plans. However, anxiety is only useful when it is a temporary emotion, not when it is all-consuming. Constant or intense anxiety causes stress and can interfere with daily functioning. Psychologist Cheryl Carmin describes the difference this way: "Most people are anxious before a job interview, but for the person who has an anxiety disorder, they may cancel the interview altogether due to their fear about what the interviewer may think about them."[6] Anxiety disorders are diagnosed when anxiety is persistent, is pervasive, and interferes with daily activities and relationships.

> "Most people are anxious before a job interview, but for the person who has an anxiety disorder, they may cancel the interview altogether due to their fear about what the interviewer may think about them."[6]
>
> – Cheryl Carmin, psychologist

MENTAL DISORDERS

Anxiety disorders are a type of mental disorder. Mental disorders are very real medical conditions. Unlike many physical illnesses, however, many mental disorders do not have a known biological cause such as a virus or gene mutation. Mental disorders are defined by their symptoms and effects, not by their causes. In general, there is no blood test or brain scan that can determine whether a person has a mental disorder. There are, however, predictable patterns to the mental distress that people feel with intense anxiety. Mental health professionals describe and define disorders by finding these patterns. They look for groups of people who experience similar symptoms in similar ways over time. They try to determine if these symptoms occur in enough people to qualify as a syndrome, or consistent group of symptoms.

In the United States, the standard text for defining and explaining mental disorders is called the *Diagnostic and Statistical Manual of Mental Disorders, 5th Edition*, or *DSM-5*. The *DSM-5* was published in 2013. It explains that "a mental disorder is a syndrome characterized by clinically significant disturbance in an individual's cognition, emotion regulation, or behavior that reflects a dysfunction in the psychological, biological, or developmental processes underlying mental functioning."[7] In other words, a mental disorder is a pattern of symptoms that has a serious negative effect. The *DSM-5* also points out that mental disorders make it significantly more difficult for a person to live life. Not all unusual behavior is mentally disordered. For instance, people with social anxiety tend to isolate themselves. However, some people decide to spend large amounts of time alone because of religious practice or personal preference, not social anxiety. In addition, sometimes people go through times of extreme mental distress because of difficult life experiences, like the death of a loved one. Mental disorders, by contrast, cause a lot of suffering even during normal phases of life.

TYPES OF ANXIETY DISORDERS

The *DSM-5* lists eleven different types of anxiety disorder. For each of the listed anxiety disorders, anxiety is the primary symptom that patients experience. People with different anxiety disorders may fear different things, but they all experience excessive fear and worry as the main cause of their distress. In general, the person must be suffering from disordered levels of anxiety for six months in order to be diagnosed with an anxiety disorder.

The most common anxiety disorder is specific phobias, followed by social anxiety disorder and generalized anxiety disorder. The other anxiety disorders recognized by the *DSM-5* are panic disorder, agoraphobia, separation anxiety disorder, selective mutism, substance/medication-induced anxiety disorder, anxiety disorder due to another medical condition, other specified anxiety disorder, and unspecified anxiety disorder.

SPECIFIC PHOBIAS

The word *phobia* comes from the ancient Greek word for fear. A phobia is a particular kind of fear. Phobias can be fears of objects, people and animals, places, or situations. A phobia is distinguished from a regular fear by its strength and irrationality. For example, it's common and reasonable to be afraid of heights. Falls can be dangerous, and feeling nervous at high altitudes can help people stay cautious and alert. However, people with a phobia of heights will feel much more than self-protective fear. They will dread and fear high places to the point that life becomes more difficult. They may start to avoid everyday encounters, like a meeting on the fourth floor of a building, because of the phobia. Many people with specific phobia disorder first experience their phobia in childhood.

The cause of a phobia is not always clear. Common phobias include acrophobia (fear of heights), arachnophobia (fear of spiders), and coulrophobia (fear of clowns).

Jessica, who did not share her last name, developed her phobia of vomiting and being sick as a child. "As I grew up, I knew there was a problem," Jessica remembers. "I couldn't watch any medical [shows] on TV without having to cover up my eyes . . . and I was constantly worried that I was going to be ill too."[8]

Sometimes, people develop phobias after a traumatic experience. For instance, a person who is bitten by a dog as a child may end up having a phobia of dogs. In many cases, specific phobias develop for no clear reason. Three-quarters of people with specific phobia anxiety disorder have more than one phobia. About 7 to 9 percent of Americans have a specific phobia at any given time.

SOCIAL ANXIETY DISORDER

People with social anxiety disorder have serious worries and fears about being judged by others. According to the *DSM-5*, a person with social anxiety disorder "is concerned that he or she will be judged as anxious, weak, crazy, stupid, boring, intimidating, dirty, or unlikable."[9] People with social anxiety disorder have physical symptoms of anxiety, like blushing and sweating, when they are around other people. They are so afraid of being judged by others that they may avoid social situations. Other people with social anxiety disorder become very afraid that they say or do things that offend other people. Michelle B used Twitter to share her experience of social anxiety: "My flavor of social anxiety," she wrote, "is talking to anyone and everyone easily, and then waking up at 3 a.m. with a voice going over everything I said, imagining all the ways it could be taken negatively, and then telling me how stupid I sounded and how everyone hates me now."[10] People with social anxiety disorder may come across as shy and withdrawn. They may be more likely to choose careers and lifestyles that don't require much social interaction. Most people with social anxiety disorders begin having symptoms between the ages of eight and fifteen. However, symptoms can arise at any age.

GENERALIZED ANXIETY DISORDER

People with Generalized Anxiety Disorder (GAD) feel anxiety in a variety of contexts. Their anxiety is persistent and stretches across many areas of their life. People with GAD often experience anxiety with no clear cause—in other words, they become very worried with nothing in particular to be worried about. GAD sufferers have some of the physical symptoms of anxiety, like tiredness and muscle tension. However, they are less likely to have some of the physical symptoms of panic, like a racing heart or shortness of breath, than people with other anxiety disorders are.

PERFORMANCE ANXIETY

The *DSM-5* describes a special type of social anxiety called performance-only anxiety. Performance anxiety is a type of social anxiety related to publicly doing a specific task, like giving a speech or playing in a concert. People with performance-only social anxiety may feel at ease in one-on-one social situations or in small groups, but they feel classic symptoms of anxiety in public, high-stakes situations. Research suggests that performance-only social anxiety disorder tends to be relatively mild. People who perform for a living, like athletes and musicians, are most likely to suffer from disordered levels of performance-only social anxiety. Because professional entertainers have to face the stress of performing on a regular basis, and because they depend on these performances, performance anxiety is more likely to interfere with their career.

Adele is a singer who has worked professionally for over a decade. She is one of the most successful musicians of her era. Her albums sell millions of copies and she tours worldwide to huge audiences. Adele has become very successful in spite of performance anxiety that makes singing in front of people difficult. "I'm scared of audiences," she once told reporters. "One show in Amsterdam, I was so nervous I escaped out the fire exit." Adele has panic attacks sometimes while on tour. Actor Hugh Grant and singer Barbra Streisand are among the many other performers who also struggle with severe performance anxiety.

Quoted in Sabrina Felson, "Celebrities with Anxiety," WebMD, July 21, 2018. http://webmd.com.

There is overlap between the symptoms of GAD and those of other anxiety disorders. For example, a person with GAD may also suffer from social anxiety. Unlike a person who only experiences social anxiety, a person with GAD would experience elevated anxiety in many situations—not just social ones. Additionally, although a person with GAD may also suffer from occasional panic attacks, persistent general anxiety would be the main feature of this disorder—not the panic attacks.

It's common for people to start seeing symptoms of GAD in young adulthood. However, children can suffer from GAD as well. Quinn, who chose not to share their last name, began suffering from GAD at age seven. Their first anxiety symptoms were physical. They felt sick to their stomach every morning and missed school because of their nausea. Quinn remembers, "My anxiety caused me to suffer from lack of sleep due to all the 'what if' questions. . . . I missed the enjoyment of a normal childhood due to constant worrying."[11] Parents with generalized anxiety disorder also face difficulties. Adults with GAD are so troubled by worry that it is difficult for them to pass on feelings of confidence and security to others, including their children.

> "I missed the enjoyment of a normal childhood due to constant worrying."[11]
>
> – Quinn, GAD sufferer

PANIC ATTACKS AND PANIC DISORDER

A panic attack is an overwhelming experience of physical and mental fear and anxiety. Panic attacks usually last for just a few minutes, but they can feel as if they are lasting much longer. Panic attacks include at least four symptoms felt at the same time.

Several of the symptoms of panic attacks are physical. A common panic attack symptom is a feeling of a pounding or racing heart. People may also feel that they can't catch their breath or are being smothered. They may feel chest pain or tightness. Nausea is a common panic attack symptom. People having panic attacks may start to sweat, tremble, and feel dizzy and light-headed. They may feel chilled or overheated. In addition, panic attack sufferers may start to feel paresthesia, or tingling and numbness in the body.

A panic attack also affects the sufferer's thinking and perception of reality. During a panic attack, sufferers may think that they are losing control of themselves or that they are about to die. People may begin to feel like the world around them is unreal, or that they are somehow separating from themselves. This feeling of separation has a name. Feeling separated from the world is called *derealization*. Feeling separate from oneself is called *depersonalization*.

People who have panic attacks often report that they feel as if they are having a fatal heart attack. Lisa Jakub worked as a child actor from the age of four. When she was eleven, she began working on a TV show that filmed in front of a live audience. She was used to being watched, but seeing all the people at the studio was overwhelming. "Suddenly, it was like someone removed all the air from the room," Jakub remembered. "My vision got fuzzy and my hands went numb. My heart was pounding so hard I could taste it. I wondered if I was dying."[12] Jakub began suffering from panic attacks more regularly. There are unexpected and expected panic attacks. Some people know that a certain trigger, like exposure to a phobia, will result in a panic attack. Other panic attacks happen with no predictable cause.

Anyone can have a panic attack. People who do not have anxiety disorders may still suffer a few panic attacks over the course of their lives, and they can be a symptom of any kind of anxiety disorder. For people with panic disorder, however, panic attacks are the primary anxiety symptom. People must have unexpected panic attacks in order to be diagnosed with the disorder, although they may suffer from expected panic attacks as well. For panic disorder sufferers, these attacks are recurrent. They may happen on a regular basis or in

> "My vision got fuzzy and my hands went numb. My heart was pounding so hard I could taste it. I wondered if I was dying."[12]
>
> – Lisa Jakub, describing a panic attack

Agoraphobia includes the fear of open spaces. People with agoraphobia are often scared to leave their home.

short bursts with lulls in between. Even the fear of having a panic attack can trigger a panic attack. People with panic disorder have an increased risk of considering and attempting suicide.

AGORAPHOBIA

People with agoraphobia fear being trapped in closed or unfamiliar places or being overwhelmed by crowds. The *DSM-5* defines agoraphobia as an intense fear of being in at least two of five situations: on public transportation, in an open space, in an enclosed space, alone outside, or in a line or crowd. These fears share a common dread of open, public spaces or places where it's easy to get trapped. People with agoraphobia are vulnerable to panic attacks and may avoid going out in order to avoid feeling panic in public. About one-third of agoraphobia sufferers do not leave their homes. People with agoraphobia are at risk of developing substance abuse problems as they seek a way to deal with their distress. Writer and comedian Sara Benincasa suffered from agoraphobia for several years. "I was so ill with agoraphobia and suicidal depression that I was afraid to leave my room, much less my apartment," Benincasa remembers. "I couldn't ride in a car. Planes were out of the question."[13] She was unable to leave her bed at the worst period of her illness.

As with all anxiety disorders, the exact cause of agoraphobia is unknown. However, the disorder is strongly heritable, which means that people with agoraphobic parents are much more likely to develop agoraphobia themselves. Many people with agoraphobia describe their parents as cold or overprotective. There is also evidence that suffering from stressful childhood events increases the risk of agoraphobia.

SEPARATION ANXIETY DISORDER

For people with separation anxiety disorder, being away from loved ones is the main source of anxiety. People with separation anxiety may refuse to leave home or spend time alone without the people closest to them. They may have nightmares or obsessive thoughts about something terrible happening to a loved one, and they may insist on being in touch with others at all times. Separation anxiety is the most common anxiety disorder in children. For children to be diagnosed with separation anxiety and other anxiety disorders, they must show symptoms for four weeks. This differs from adults, who must show symptoms for six months. Adults are significantly less likely than children to suffer from separation anxiety.

However, about 1 to 2 percent of people over eighteen have the disorder. Adults with separation anxiety disorder are also likely to worry too much about friends and loved ones. The disorder can have severe negative effects. Allison Forti is an assistant professor of counseling. She points out that separation anxiety disorder can make adults less likely to travel for opportunities and can lead them to behave in ways that drive others away. "For adults, separation anxiety disorder . . . could lead to social isolation, loss of employment opportunities or the ability to prosper at work, relational difficulties, or the [loss of the] ability to live a satisfying and fulfilling life," Forti says.[14]

SELECTIVE MUTISM

Mutism is an inability or unwillingness to speak. People with selective mutism are able to speak in some situations but lose the ability to speak in situations that cause them anxiety. For example, a person with selective mutism may be able to speak easily around trusted friends and family members but be unable to speak in school.

Most people with selective mutism develop the disorder in early childhood. Anna Clark, who has selective mutism, remembers that she lost the ability to speak at age six. "I can see myself sitting with the teacher in my classroom," Clark wrote. "She wanted me to read out loud to her, but I couldn't. I was frozen."[15] Selective mutism is rare, with fewer than 1 percent of US children suffering from the disorder. For many children with selective mutism, symptoms do not progress into adulthood.

> "I can see myself sitting with the teacher in my classroom. She wanted me to read out loud to her, but I couldn't. I was frozen."[15]
>
> – Anna Clark, selective mutism sufferer

SUBSTANCE/MEDICATION-INDUCED ANXIETY DISORDER

Substance/medication-induced anxiety disorders occur when a person ingests something that causes anxiety. The substances can include drugs like caffeine and cocaine, as well as heavy metals, toxic gases like carbon monoxide, and some medications. This disorder is only diagnosed when it is clear that a substance is directly contributing to anxiety symptoms. If the symptoms persist long after the person stops using the substance, it is not a substance-induced anxiety disorder. For example, a daily coffee drinker might decide to give up caffeine after experiencing generalized anxiety. If his panic and worry continued one month after quitting the drug, he would not be diagnosed with this disorder.

ANXIETY DISORDER DUE TO ANOTHER MEDICAL CONDITION

There are several diseases and disorders that often cause anxiety. Some endocrine (hormone), cardiovascular (heart), respiratory (breathing), and neurological (nervous system) illnesses and disorders result in anxiety symptoms. Deficiencies or excessive amounts of substances like vitamins can also lead to anxiety. Mental health professionals and physicians can collaborate to diagnose this anxiety disorder when it is clear that the patient's anxiety has one of these underlying medical causes.

OTHER SPECIFIED ANXIETY DISORDER AND UNSPECIFIED ANXIETY DISORDER

Sometimes mental health providers diagnose an anxiety disorder that does not exactly fit the symptoms of any of these anxiety disorders. The anxiety may present itself slightly differently or fit only some of the criteria. In these cases, the patient may be diagnosed with other specified anxiety

OBSESSIVE-COMPULSIVE DISORDER AND PTSD

The *DSM-5* reorganized the classifications of several mental disorders. Two common mental disorders, obsessive-compulsive disorder (OCD) and post-traumatic stress disorder (PTSD), were previously defined as anxiety disorders. In the *DSM-5*, they are grouped differently. However, the symptoms of OCD and PTSD overlap with those of anxiety disorders.

OCD is a mental disorder defined by repeating, unstoppable thoughts (obsessions) and behaviors (compulsions). People with OCD find themselves unable to control some of their thoughts and actions and may find themselves repeating certain actions, like turning off a faucet over and over again in order to feel safe. People with OCD might try to alleviate anxious thoughts with certain behaviors or rituals. Patients often feel ashamed about the way they think and act. In the *DSM-5*, OCD falls under the larger category of obsessive-compulsive and related disorders.

People with PTSD have lived through or witnessed a trauma, or deeply harmful life event. Sexual assault, military combat, and physical abuse are examples of trauma. People with PTSD may have physical and mental symptoms of anxiety or panic attacks when they remember the trauma. The disorder is now grouped with trauma- and stressor-related disorders.

disorder. Health care providers make this diagnosis when a patient has symptoms of an anxiety disorder but there is not enough information available to be more specific. For example, sometimes a doctor sees a patient for only a few minutes before referring them to someone else. The doctor may observe that the patient is suffering from clinical anxiety but not know its exact cause and presentation.

There is also a great deal of variety within each anxiety disorder. Every patient thinks, acts, and experiences symptoms differently. For this reason, the diagnosis of anxiety disorders is a complicated process. Medical professionals, mental health professionals, and patients work together to explore symptoms, rule out other diagnoses, and understand how the disorder is affecting the patient's life.

ANXIETY
IN THE BRAIN

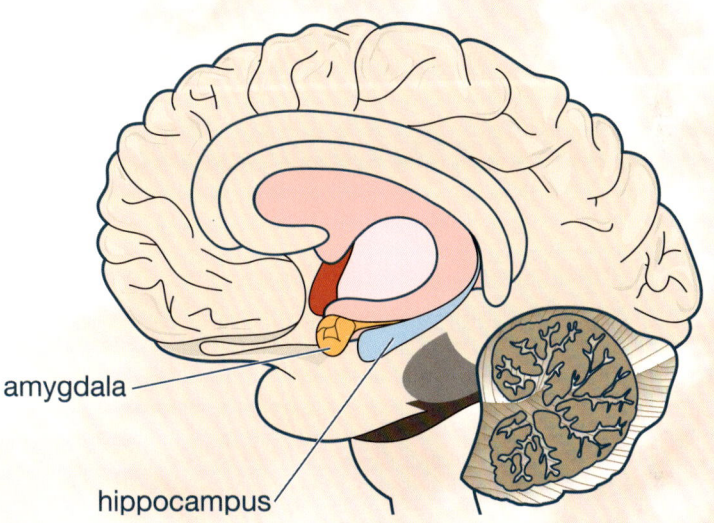

Two key parts of the brain play a role in most anxiety disorders. They are the amygdala and the hippocampus. Scientists believe the amygdala is a communications center in the brain. It processes and interprets incoming sensory signals. The amygdala tells the rest of the brain when it detects a threat. This triggers a physical fear response.

The hippocampus is responsible for creating memories. Scientists have found that the hippocampus is smaller in victims of trauma such as child abuse or combat.

"Anxiety," Cook Counseling, November 2013. http://cookcounselingmn.com.

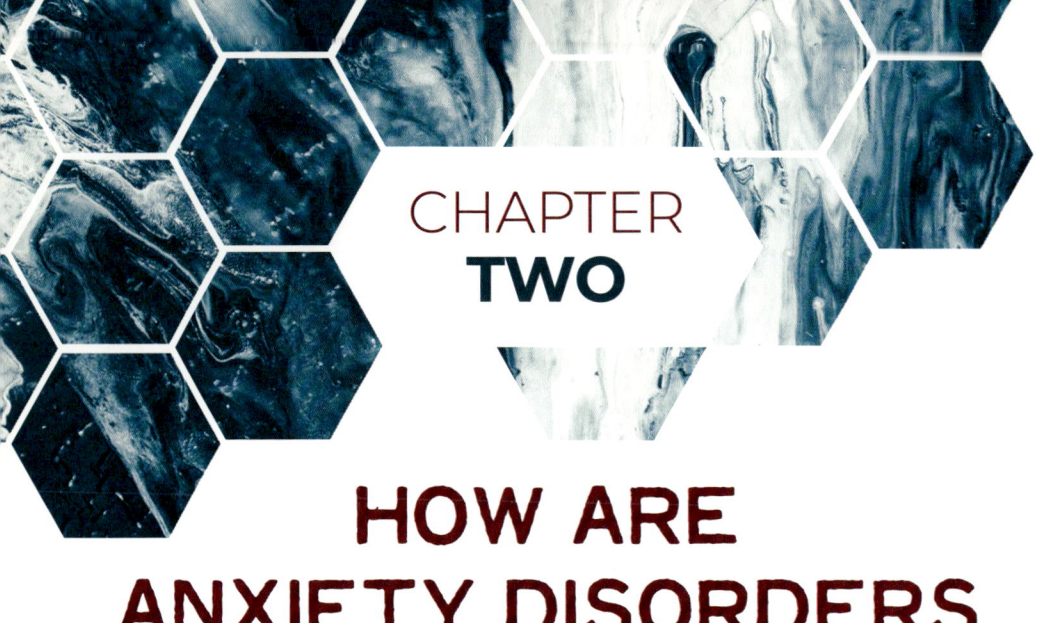

CHAPTER TWO

HOW ARE ANXIETY DISORDERS DIAGNOSED?

In the United States, the *DSM-5* is the standard resource for helping medical professionals define and diagnose mental disorders. The *DSM-5* is the fifth edition of the *Diagnostic and Statistical Manual of Mental Disorders*. The *DSM-III*, published in 1980, marked a shift from previous versions of the manual. It was more detailed in outlining symptoms of each disorder and instructing professionals on how to diagnose them.

These detailed diagnostic criteria led to a great deal of disagreement about how and when to distinguish between different mental disorders. In order to manage these differences, the *DSM* is written by committee. Before making a new edition of the *DSM*, the American Psychological Association (APA) forms work groups. These groups research each mental disorder and write reports summarizing what they find. They think about whether current definitions of mental disorders truly describe the symptoms people suffer from in real life. Then, other groups of medical

Mental health professionals use the *DSM-5* to diagnose mental disorders. It provides the criteria necessary for a diagnosis.

professionals work to revise old diagnoses and write new ones as needed. The *DSM* is mostly written by psychiatrists, but psychologists and other healthcare providers contribute as well. More than 160 people served on the groups that researched and revised the manual, while more than 300 others gave expert advice. In addition, the APA opened some parts of the writing process for public review. People from outside the mental health profession were able to read and comment on the descriptions of various mental disorders.

THE HISTORY OF ANXIETY DISORDERS

The mental disorders researched and described by the *DSM* are only about four decades old. Current understandings of mental disorders have their roots in the invention of psychoanalysis in the nineteenth century, the behavioral model of the nineteenth and twentieth centuries, and the twentieth century's medical model of mental disorders.

In the late nineteenth century, Austrian psychiatrist Sigmund Freud developed several theories about the function of the mind and the causes of mental distress. Freud believed that people had subconscious desires, often sexual or violent desires, that they had learned to suppress in childhood. According to Freud, people felt great guilt and shame about having these desires and tried to deny them. This denial resulted in anxiety. Freud developed the technique of psychoanalysis, where patients meet with a doctor to discuss their inner feelings and memories. Psychoanalysis was adopted and changed by many other doctors and psychologists. It is the ancestor of the various forms of modern talk therapy. Freud later changed his ideas about the sources of anxiety. However, his core ideas about anxiety as driven by painful, often hidden feelings and memories were very influential.

BEHAVIORAL PSYCHOLOGY

According to professor of sociology Allan Horwitz, "During the first six decades of the twentieth century, psychoanalytic approaches dominated the study of anxiety within psychiatry."[16] However, around the time of World War II (1939–1945), many psychologists and psychiatrists began to

ANXIETY DISORDERS IN ANIMALS

Like humans, some animals suffer from anxiety disorders. Household pets like dogs and cats are often observed as having separation anxiety disorder. Pets with separation anxiety dread being left alone by their owners. They act out their fears and worries by doing things like urinating indoors, chewing obsessively, or barking for attention. They will look out for signs that they are going to be left alone and act out to get their owner's attention and care. They may also try to break out of the house to find their owners. Just like humans, some animals are at elevated risk for separation anxiety disorder. Animals who have experienced traumas like abandonment by a previous owner may be more likely to have separation anxiety. In addition, some types of animals, like smaller dog breeds, tend to be at higher risk of disordered anxiety levels.

Veterinarians can diagnose separation anxiety based on a pet's behavior and recommend several courses of action. Pets and owners can work together to develop new behavior responses that help reduce the effects of anxiety. For example, an owner might start leaving the house for very short times, and then slowly increase the lengths of separation from the pet. For more severe cases of separation anxiety disorder, the vet may prescribe an anti-anxiety medication.

Pets also respond to lifestyle changes like increased activity. For example, giving a dog many different "jobs" to do, like walking or chasing balls, can help ease anxiety disorder symptoms.

---

study large groups of people using personality tests, psychological trials, and other forms of research. Their goal was to collect information about the ways people tend to act in various situations, including combat. One of the main ideas behind behavioral psychology was that people learned how to think and behave based on their past experiences.

These psychologists drew on the work of Russian scientist Ivan Pavlov. Pavlov studied how animals learned to adjust their behavior to their environment. He studied dogs' physical responses to the things they observed in their lives. In his most famous experiment, he gave dogs some food every time he used a certain buzzer. Over time, the dogs began to salivate when they heard the buzzer, even when there was no food around. The dogs did not have any natural instinct to feel hungry at the sound of a buzzer. Instead, they had learned to associate the sound with food over time. Pavlov's work helped introduce the idea that it's possible to adjust behavior even without consciously choosing to. He helped shape the field of behavioral psychology. In the early twentieth century, behavioral psychologists began to look at how and why people took on certain phobias. They imagined that phobias in humans might work a little like drooling in dogs. If people had negative memories of an object or experience, they would learn over time to associate that object or experience with intense fear. Behavioral psychology had certain weaknesses, however. For example, it could not explain how people developed phobias of seemingly random objects. Behavioral psychology also had no answer for why phobias persisted even though people knew from experience that the feared object was not dangerous. In other words, it could not explain why people struggled to unlearn certain thoughts and behaviors.

In the 1950s, the medical model of thinking about anxiety disorders became more popular. This theory suggested that mental disorders like anxiety were caused by problems in the brain. More specifically, doctors proposed that mental disorders arose from chemical imbalances like too much or too little of hormones that regulate stress. Pharmaceutical companies developed some of the first anti-anxiety medications around this time. These drugs were widely prescribed for a variety of mental illnesses. Most psychiatric medications were not prescribed for specific mental disorders. Many people criticized medical doctors for giving drugs to people who were dealing with the stresses of everyday life rather than a diagnosed mental disorder. The APA developed an official system for describing anxiety disorders that helped change this.

THE FIRST *DSM*

The APA released the first *Diagnostic and Statistical Manual of Mental Disorders* in 1952. The *DSM* was unique in that it focused on disorders in the general population, not just in hospitalized people. This first manual defined anxiety as the main feature of "neurosis."[17] The modern definition of anxiety disorder dates to the *DSM-III*, which was published in 1980. The *DSM-IV*, published in 1994, clarified the definitions of many disorders. It also added and subtracted several disorders. The APA worked to make sure that the disorders it described were supported by research.

As of the early twenty-first century, most anxiety experts propose an explanation for anxiety disorders that falls somewhere in between the psychoanalytic, behavioral, and medical models. Mental health professionals tend to understand anxiety as arising from a mix of factors, including biology and personal emotions and experiences. Some people's bodies and brains may be set up in such a way that they are more likely to develop anxiety. Others are raised in or live in environments that make anxiety more likely or have feelings and experiences that trigger anxiety. Emotions, behavior, and biology are constantly affecting each other throughout an individual's life. In the words of psychologist Carolyn Daitch, "An interaction between genetic and environmental factors influences how we think, develop, and experience life."[18]

> "An interaction between genetic and environmental factors influences how we think, develop, and experience life."[18]
>
> – Psychologist Carolyn Daitch

Self-screening tools can help people learn more about their symptoms. People can decide if it's time to see a mental health professional.

SELF-SCREENING FOR ANXIETY DISORDERS

There are resources available for people who aren't sure if they should seek treatment for anxiety. When people like Lixi want to understand more about the anxiety they're feeling, they can turn to screening tools.

The National Alliance on Mental Illness (NAMI) offers a free text and telephone helpline. People who call the helpline can ask questions about their symptoms and get referrals to health care providers. The ADAA and

Mental Health America are two organizations that offer self-screening tools for abnormal levels of anxiety. These tools are tests that ask people to list their anxiety symptoms and describe how severe they are and how long they've been going on.

Self-screening tools can give people some perspectives on their symptoms and help them recognize the need to see a professional. But they aren't substitutes for an official diagnosis. The most important step is a trip to a qualified health care provider.

FINDING A HEALTH CARE PROVIDER

Several types of health care providers treat anxiety disorders. Psychiatrists are medical doctors who diagnose and treat mental, emotional, and behavioral disorders. They can make diagnoses, prescribe medicine, and lead therapy sessions. Other medical doctors, like primary care doctors, can also diagnose mental disorders and prescribe medication to treat them. However, doctors who do not specialize in psychiatry will usually not give long-term treatment or therapy for anxiety disorders.

Psychologists receive doctoral degrees in psychology and also diagnose disorders and lead therapy sessions. However, in most US states, psychologists do not prescribe medicine. Some social workers specialize in psychotherapy and mental disorders. These social workers receive master's degrees and can usually diagnose mental disorders, although they do not prescribe medication.

For many people, finding a social worker, psychiatrist, or psychologist can be a daunting task. Often, an easier step is to go to a primary care doctor. During a normal checkup, primary care doctors can ask questions about symptoms of mental disorders. However, it is best not to see a primary care doctor for long-term treatment. As the National Institute of Mental Health (NIMH) points out, "Historically, it has been difficult for a primary care provider alone to offer effective, high quality behavioral health care."[19] Instead, the primary care doctor can make referrals, or recommendations about other health care providers. A primary care doctor will give good advice about which mental health care provider would be best to see next.

THE DIAGNOSTIC PROCESS

Health care providers cannot give a simple test to decide if someone has an anxiety disorder. Instead, they must talk with the patient to understand the scope and severity of the patient's symptoms. They might gather information from a physical exam, a series of conversations, and their observations of the patient.

The *DSM-5* provides a list of symptoms that define each of the anxiety disorders. However, not every person with an anxiety disorder experiences the same symptoms in the same way. For example, a patient like Lixi, who suspects she has GAD, may explain her symptoms to the psychiatrist her doctor has referred her to. The psychiatrist would listen to her describe her experiences, ask follow-up questions, and make his own observations. The psychiatrist knows that the *DSM-5* lists six symptoms that define the syndrome of Generalized Anxiety Disorder. The symptoms are feelings of restlessness or being on edge, feeling easily tired, difficulty concentrating, irritability, muscle tension, and a variety of sleep troubles, such as insomnia or poor sleep, grouped under the term *sleep disturbance*.

A patient only needs to be suffering from three of the given symptoms, most days of the week, for six months in order to qualify for a diagnosis of

Sleep disturbance is one of six official symptoms of GAD. To be diagnosed with GAD, a person must experience at least three of the six symptoms more days than not for a period of six months.

GAD. During the course of their conversation, the psychiatrist might find that while Lixi does have trouble sleeping, is on edge, feels tired, and finds it hard to concentrate, she does not feel irritable and her muscles feel fine. This would not disqualify her for a diagnosis of GAD, as she has four of the six symptoms.

DIFFERENTIAL DIAGNOSES

Before settling on a diagnosis, however, mental health care providers must take a close look at other conditions and illnesses with similar symptoms. It is important to make sure that the diagnosis is accurate and that the patient does not suffer from a different condition with similar features. This is called making a differential diagnosis.

The *DSM-5* lists differential diagnoses for each mental disorder. In some cases, people may present with anxiety symptoms that have a clear physical cause. For example, hyperthyroidism is an illness that occurs when the body produces too much thyroid hormone. Hyperthyroidism shares several key symptoms with GAD, including irritability, sleep trouble, and anxiety. Although the symptoms are the same, treatments for hyperthyroidism and GAD have key differences. A mental health professional might want to do thyroid tests to rule out the condition before moving forward with a diagnosis of GAD.

In addition, since almost all anxiety disorders have overlapping symptoms, mental health care providers must make differential diagnoses among other mental disorders. For example, in her meeting with a psychiatrist, Lixi might stress how nervous she's been feeling around other people at school and how much she dreads seeing friends. These symptoms are classic signs of social anxiety disorder. In order to decide between social anxiety disorder and GAD, the psychiatrist would need to think carefully about whether Lixi's symptoms are linked mostly to social situations or occur in other contexts. The *DSM-5* guides health care providers in distinguishing between the two disorders. "Individuals with social anxiety disorder often have anticipatory anxiety that is focused on upcoming social situations in which they must perform or be evaluated by others," the text points out, "whereas individuals with generalized anxiety disorder worry, whether or not they are being evaluated."[20]

PSYCHOEDUCATION

Once a medical professional has decided on a diagnosis, she can inform the patient on the condition and give options for treatment. This explanation process is called psychoeducation. Psychoeducation is a vital step in the diagnostic process. In the words of psychologist Carolyn Daitch, "Clients need to be provided with an understanding of their styles of reactivity, symptoms, and the effect on their functioning."[21] In other words, two people with the same anxiety disorder may suffer from different symptoms and feel the effects of their disorder differently. Psychoeducation helps patients understand the specifics of how their disorder affects their lives. It also helps them realize that they are not alone.

A clear, understandable diagnosis helps patients understand what they are going through and that they are not alone. Writer Tracy Clayton suffered from anxiety for years before being diagnosed with GAD. For her, having a name for the symptoms she was experiencing was freeing and encouraging. It also encouraged her to seek help for her condition. "I stopped blaming myself for my shortcomings, because it felt to me like the equivalent of blaming yourself for having the flu," Clayton wrote. "When you get sick, you don't just will yourself to get better."[22]

> "Individuals with social anxiety disorder often have anticipatory anxiety that is focused on upcoming social situations in which they must perform or be evaluated by others, whereas individuals with generalized anxiety disorder worry, whether or not they are being evaluated."[20]
>
> – *The DSM-5, on the difference between social anxiety disorder and GAD*

The World Health Organization reported in 2015 that 3.6 percent of the world's population suffers from an anxiety disorder. Women are more likely than men to be diagnosed.

RISK FACTORS FOR ANXIETY DISORDERS

Not everyone suffers equally from anxiety disorders. Women are much more likely to be diagnosed with anxiety disorders than men are. Up to age fifty, women are twice as likely to be diagnosed with an anxiety disorder. There are a few possible reasons why women have higher rates of clinical anxiety. One proposed explanation is that biological differences between men's and women's brains make women more vulnerable to anxiety. According to the ADAA, women's higher levels of the hormones estrogen and progesterone make them more likely to experience the physical and emotional symptoms of anxiety, and to experience them for longer periods of time.

Another explanation is that men and women face different cultural norms and have different life experiences. For example, women are more likely to do caretaking work inside the home and may feel more responsible for others' well-being than men do. The added stress of these responsibilities may increase the risk of anxiety. It's also possible that women simply reach out for treatment more often than men.

> "I stopped blaming myself for my shortcomings, because it felt to me like the equivalent of blaming yourself for having the flu."[22]
>
> *– Writer Tracy Clayton, on the relief of being diagnosed with an anxiety disorder*

Reported rates of anxiety disorders also vary greatly among different racial and cultural groups. In the United States, white people are more likely than people of other races to be diagnosed with anxiety disorders. There are several potential reasons for these differences. There are some cultural factors that may reduce the risk of anxiety disorders. For example, a 2011 study found that for African Americans, feeling rooted in a strong sense of ethnic identity reduced the risk of anxiety. This finding suggests that in some cultures, feeling a strong sense of belonging in ethnic identity may help guard against anxiety. In addition, there are differences in the way that people perceive and discuss anxiety symptoms. Standard surveys of anxiety may not capture these variations. It is also possible that, like gender differences in rates of anxiety, these disparities are due to differences in reporting and treatment. In other words, white people may simply be more likely to access mental health treatment than people of other races.

ANXIETY AND CULTURAL CONTEXT

It's human to feel worry and fear. However, anxiety is understood and expressed differently across different places and eras. The *DSM-5*'s definitions capture a twenty-first century US view of anxiety and anxiety disorders. Anxiety disorders can vary in their symptoms, expression, and treatment depending on the culture in which they arise. For example, indigenous peoples living in the Arctic who hunted seals sometimes suffered from *kayak-svimmel*, or kayak-angst. After hours spent alone waiting for a seal in open water, a hunter might begin to feel dizzy and agitated. In kayak-svimmel, "a sensation of cold rising from below makes the hunter fear that the kayak is filling with water." The hunter might suffer a panic attack until he was able to return to land. He might also have delusional thoughts. Kayak-svimmel shares many similarities to the *DSM*'s definition of a panic attack. However, the delusional thoughts of kayak-svimmel are not characteristic of panic attacks. Furthermore, it is unlikely that someone who is not from a culture where hunting in kayaks is common would feel the exact symptoms of kayak-svimmel.

Fritz A. Henn et al., Contemporary Psychiatry, *New York: Springer, 2001, p. 224.*

According to the World Health Organization (WHO), as of 2015, about 3.6 percent of the world population suffered from an anxiety disorder. The WHO found that 23 percent of the world's anxiety disorder diagnoses came from southeast Asia. This was followed by 21 percent from the Americas and 20 percent from the western Pacific region. The WHO estimates that in the Americas, 7.7 percent of women and 3.6 percent of men have anxiety disorders. Symptoms of anxiety disorders vary from culture to culture. For example, in some parts of the world, people with GAD experience more of the physical symptoms of anxiety, like headaches and muscle tension, while in other places, worry and upsetting thoughts are the main symptoms.

In addition, some life experiences make people more likely to suffer from certain anxiety disorders. People with overprotective parents may be more likely to develop anxiety disorders. People who experience childhood trauma such as abuse grow up with chronic stress, making them vulnerable to anxiety.

ANXIETY AND OTHER HEALTH CONDITIONS

In some cases, anxiety disorders are correlated with increased incidence of other illnesses and disorders. The word *correlated* means "associated." In many cases, it is unclear what the exact relationship between two disorders is. For example, people with autism spectrum disorder are more likely than other people to have an anxiety disorder. However, this does not mean that autism causes anxiety, or that anxiety causes autism. The relationship between the two may be very complicated. Anxiety disorders are strongly correlated with major depressive disorder, another common mental disorder. People with major depressive disorder, sometimes called clinical depression, have sadness and low moods that persist and make normal life difficult. Like anxiety sufferers, people with depression may have trouble sleeping and may suffer from fatigue and irritability. There is significant overlap between the populations of people who suffer from anxiety disorders and clinical depression. In fact, almost half of people with one of these disorders also suffer from the other one.

Mental health professionals are not sure why anxiety and depression occur together so often. It's possible that very stressful life events can trigger both depression and anxiety at the same time. It may also be that anxiety and depression have similar biological risk factors. Anxiety and depression can be comorbid, or co-occurring, in many different ways. Some people may sense that their depression is more severe than their anxiety. Others may feel that the stresses of an anxiety disorder make them more likely to become depressed. Ismail T. wrote about his

Anxiety is often comorbid with depression. Depression can make the symptoms of anxiety more difficult to manage.

experiences with depression and anxiety: "Depression is not caring about anything at all, and anxiety is caring too much. And having both, ironically, is a nightmare. You want to leave everything behind and sleep, yet you overthink anxiously about everything you didn't or have to do."[23]

Rebecca Jane Stokes, who suffers from both anxiety and depression, points out that both anxiety and depression make it difficult for people to take care of themselves, in different ways. When she is depressed, Stokes writes, "I neglect myself." When she is in a state of anxiety, she says, "It can actually keep me from getting real work done."[24] Anxiety and depression can be harder to treat when they are comorbid.

> "Depression is not caring about anything at all, and anxiety is caring too much. And having both, ironically, is a nightmare."[23]
>
> – Ismail T., on suffering from both anxiety and depression

The understanding, definition, and diagnosis of anxiety disorders have all changed a great deal in a short amount of time. Today, most medical professionals understand anxiety disorders as syndromes with biological, genetic, and environmental causes. Health care professionals diagnose anxiety disorders by learning about patients' symptoms and finding a diagnosis that best explains them. But the diagnostic process doesn't end there. Health care providers must also help patients learn about the way the disorder affects them personally and watch out for comorbid conditions like depression.

> "I neglect myself. . . . it can actually keep me from getting real work done."[24]
>
> –Rebecca Jane Stokes on the difficulties of comorbid anxiety and depression

CHAPTER
THREE

WHAT IS LIFE LIKE WITH ANXIETY DISORDERS?

Anxiety disorders reach every aspect of sufferers' lives. They affect personal health, the ability to function, and relationships with others. Anxiety disorders don't just make everyday life more difficult and painful. They can also profoundly affect a person's ability to live a full life and achieve their most important goals.

THE PHYSICAL TOLL OF ANXIETY

Chronic anxiety is harmful to the body. Common symptoms like headaches, muscle tension, and dizziness make it more difficult to function in daily life. Anxiety disorders can lead to long-term problems with sleep. The effects of poor sleep include irritability and lack of focus. Sleeplessness makes people more likely to get sick. It can also make anxiety more pronounced.

In addition, anxiety disorders are linked to illnesses of the lungs and digestive system. People with irritable bowel syndrome (IBS) suffer

Anxiety has both physical and mental effects. Anxiety can be linked to illnesses in the heart, lungs, and digestive system.

from stomach pain and uncomfortable symptoms like constipation and diarrhea. IBS is linked to stress, and the relationship between IBS and anxiety disorders can travel in both directions. Research suggests that if people with anxiety get a bowel infection, they are more likely to get IBS. In addition, people with IBS suffer from increased anxiety due to the stress and discomfort of the condition.

Anxiety disorders and breathing disorders interact with each other in a similar way. Chronic obstructive pulmonary disease (COPD) is a lung disease that makes it difficult for people to breathe deeply. For people with anxiety disorders who also have trouble taking even, deep breaths, COPD is especially dangerous. Anxiety worsens the symptoms of COPD, and experiencing COPD can make people feel very anxious. Clinical social worker Caryn Blanton works on the mental health of ill patients. "When our breath becomes shallow, our brains can sometimes perceive there to be a stressful situation at hand, even when there isn't," Blanton explains.[25] For people with COPD, having an anxiety disorder is a dangerous complicating risk factor.

People with anxiety disorders often feel the effects of fear and panic in their hearts—a racing, fluttering heartbeat is a sign that something's wrong. Some researchers believe that over time, these irregular heart patterns can lead to more permanent heart problems. There is evidence that anxiety can increase the risk of heart disease and heart attack. Dr. Una McCann, a psychiatrist who studies anxiety, believes that anxiety disorders have a strong relationship to heart disease. While the research on the topic is incomplete, McCann believes that anxiety can affect heart disease "both as a contributing factor and as an obstacle in recovery."[26] In other words, anxiety plays multiple harmful roles. Not only can it make heart disease more likely, it can get in the way of patients' efforts to heal.

In patients with other illnesses and conditions, anxiety disorders can also slow down the healing and recovery process. A 2011 study published in *Immunology and Allergy Clinics of North America* found that psychological stresses like anxiety slow down the healing process in patients with wounds like stitches after surgery. In fact, the patients with the highest levels of depression and anxiety were four times more likely to heal slowly than other patients. In addition, patients with more anxiety

ALCOHOL ABUSE AND SOCIAL ANXIETY

One old nickname related to alcohol is "liquid courage." The name reflects the truth that drinking alcohol lowers inhibitions. Inhibitions are the thoughts and worries that hold people back from certain behaviors. For people with anxiety, alcohol's ability to remove worries makes it a powerful drug. Alcohol is also a common part of many social gatherings and traditions. People with an anxiety disorder may find themselves turning to alcohol in order to ease the worry and stress they feel around others. Over time, they may come to rely on alcohol to help with anxiety. This type of dependence on alcohol as a treatment for painful symptoms is called *self-medication*. Using alcohol to soothe anxiety comes with serious risks and downsides. Alcohol lowers all inhibitions, including the useful ones that help keep people from behaving in inappropriate ways. People who self-medicate with alcohol may find themselves embarrassed or ashamed of the things they did while drinking. This can cause stress that leads to more anxiety. In addition, alcohol use can cause symptoms of anxiety, such as nausea or a racing heartbeat. People who self-medicate their anxiety disorders with alcohol are also at increased risk for alcohol abuse. About 1 in 5 people with social anxiety disorder abuse or depend on alcohol, according to the ADAA. Additionally, alcohol worsens the side effects of many anti-anxiety medications.

were more likely to soothe themselves by using tobacco or alcohol. These behaviors slowed down their healing progress.

NAVIGATING SOCIAL ANXIETY

Most people can remember feeling social anxiety. Being alone in a room of strangers, expecting an important phone call, giving a speech in front of peers—life is full of nerve-racking or difficult social situations. For people with social anxiety, these situations can be paralyzing instead of just difficult. Social anxiety disorder sufferers may find themselves unable to build strong relationships with others. Paul Mite began suffering from social anxiety in the late 1990s. He was deeply scared of meeting or talking with other people, which made his life very difficult. "I hid from life,"

> "I hid from life."[27]
> – Paul Mite, social anxiety sufferer

Paul remembers. For Paul, even the idea of leaving the house alone triggered anxiety. "I would stay home because I would be fearful of going out with the concern that I would potentially bump into somebody that I would know, which would bring on tremendous levels of anxiety."[27]

Social anxiety disorder can also have a devastating effect on the sufferer's sense of self. People with social anxiety disorder are often consumed with thoughts that they have done the wrong thing around other people, or that other people hate them. This constant stream of negative self-talk can make it almost impossible to have healthy self-esteem, which in turn makes relating to others even more of a struggle. People with social anxiety disorder often find themselves in a cycle of isolation and poor self-image. Justin Bayshore from the Social Anxiety Institute talked about social anxiety in a video for the website. He explained that people who suffer from social anxiety are often stuck in the belief that other people dislike them and are criticizing them at all times. "We start to believe things about ourselves that really aren't true," Justin explains. "Our anxiety just kind of tailspins and keeps getting worse and worse and worse."[28]

> "We start to believe things about ourselves that really aren't true. Our anxiety just kind of tailspins and keeps getting worse and worse and worse."[28]
> – Justin Bayshore, Social Anxiety Institute

LIVING SMALLER LIVES

All anxiety disorders have the common effect of making the world smaller and more difficult to navigate. Anxiety disorders can make everyday parts of life

Having a support system can make living with anxiety more manageable. However, some people with anxiety fear being a burden on their loved ones.

almost impossible. Laura Bartley is a writer who suffers from agoraphobia. In 2015, she hit a low point with the disorder, and her world shrank. At that time, she was only able to go to a few places besides her house. She became totally dependent on her family. She could not work or drive. She couldn't go to the store without her mom or her sister with her. She had intense panic attacks if she ventured outside her small comfort zone. Bartley felt a great deal of sadness and anger at the confines of her life. "Not only does it make everything difficult, it also makes me incredibly sad and frustrated that I cannot do the things I once could," Bartley wrote about her agoraphobia.[29]

> "Not only does it make everything difficult, it also makes me incredibly sad and frustrated that I cannot do the things I once could."[29]
>
> – *Writer Laura Bartley, on agoraphobia*

For Anna Clark, selective mutism has made it impossible to live the adult life she once hoped for. Because she cannot speak to most people, Clark depends on her mother to help her with basic life tasks. She is a grown woman and has no physical issues with speaking. But because she has never really practiced speaking to others, she doesn't have an adult's conversational skills. She does not have a job or friends and rarely leaves her home. Anna told *Vice* that she sometimes thinks of the things in life that speaking could bring her. "Maybe I would travel, maybe I would be married and have children," Anna wrote to a reporter. "I could try to make friends. I could find what my role in life is."[30]

Specific phobias can place severe limits on a sufferer's ability to experience many areas of life. For example, some people suffer from tokophobia, or the fear of pregnancy and childbirth. Giving birth can be an extremely painful, sometimes dangerous experience, and feeling nervous and scared is normal. However, people with tokophobia may reorganize their lives around this strong fear. Some women with the phobia choose never to have children because of their worries. Others may avoid not just pregnancy in themselves, but also pregnant people and images of pregnancy. A woman shared anonymously on the website Reddit about her tokophobia and the effect it had on her life. "I have panic attacks when I see other people who are pregnant, even though their pregnancies have nothing at all to do with me," she wrote. "I have panic attacks around friends who I know have recently given birth, and again this has nothing to do with me."[31]

POSTPARTUM ANXIETY

Giving birth can be a physically and emotionally difficult experience, and the arrival of a new baby in a household can be a difficult adjustment. About 10 percent of postpartum women experience postpartum anxiety. Postpartum means *after giving birth*. New mothers and others who have just given birth may experience standard anxiety symptoms such as uncontrolled worry and trouble sleeping. Postpartum anxiety (PPA) includes different types of anxiety disorders like panic disorder and generalized anxiety disorder. PPA is sometimes comorbid with postpartum depression. People who have had anxiety disorders in the past are more likely to experience PPA after giving birth. It can also develop during pregnancy. New mothers may find that PPA makes early motherhood more difficult. Mothers with PPA may struggle to bond with a new child or experience excessive separation anxiety. Catherine Birndorf is a psychiatrist who works on postpartum anxiety. Birndorf recommends that new mothers and parents with PPA follow the same treatment options as other people with anxiety disorders. Talk therapy is an option, and some medications are safe to use during pregnancy and breastfeeding.

WHEN A LOVED ONE HAS AN ANXIETY DISORDER

The friends and family of people with anxiety disorders also feel the effects of anxiety. They may find themselves worrying about a loved one's suffering and missing the full presence of an isolated person in their lives. Like Laura Bartley's family, they may have to take on extra caretaking duties for a person whose life is limited by severe anxiety.

People with anxiety disorders may be reluctant to share their experiences with the people closest to them. Their social anxiety may tell them their suffering makes them a burden on other people. People with anxiety may also worry that the

> "I have panic attacks when I see other people who are pregnant, even though their pregnancies have nothing at all to do with me."[31]
>
> – *A sufferer of tokophobia, or fear of pregnancy*

> "Being told 'get over it' is the worst ever. You wouldn't tell someone with a cold to get over it."[32]
>
> – Jackie Alvarez, social anxiety sufferer

people in their lives will doubt that their symptoms are real. They worry that others will dismiss or reject what they are feeling. "Being told 'get over it' is the worst ever," social anxiety sufferer Jackie Alvarez says. "You wouldn't tell someone with a cold to get over it."[32]

THE SOCIAL COST OF ANXIETY DISORDERS

According to the Center for Workplace Mental Health, anxiety disorders lead to an average of 4.6 lost workdays a month. People with anxiety disorders are significantly more likely than others to miss work and be less productive on the job. The World Health Organization guesses that by 2030, the world will have lost 12 billion working days to depression and anxiety disorders. These missed days of work and periods of lower productivity result in billions of dollars of economic costs. Anxiety symptoms like fatigue and trouble concentrating can make performing some jobs, like driving or surgery, more dangerous.

People with anxiety are also at increased risk of ending their own lives. According to the medical journal *Depression and Anxiety*, over 70 percent of people who have attempted suicide at some point in their lives had an anxiety disorder. Because of the strong link between suicide and anxiety, experts recommend that people with anxiety disorders also be screened for suicidal thoughts or plans.

Anxiety disorders keep people from living to their fullest and realizing their true potential. The loss of opportunity, relationships, work hours, and creative drive is a loss not just for people who suffer from anxiety, but for

People with anxiety are more likely to miss work than those who do not have anxiety. They are also more likely to attempt suicide.

their community and for the world. It is vital for people with anxiety to treat and manage their symptoms so that they can take advantage of what life has to offer.

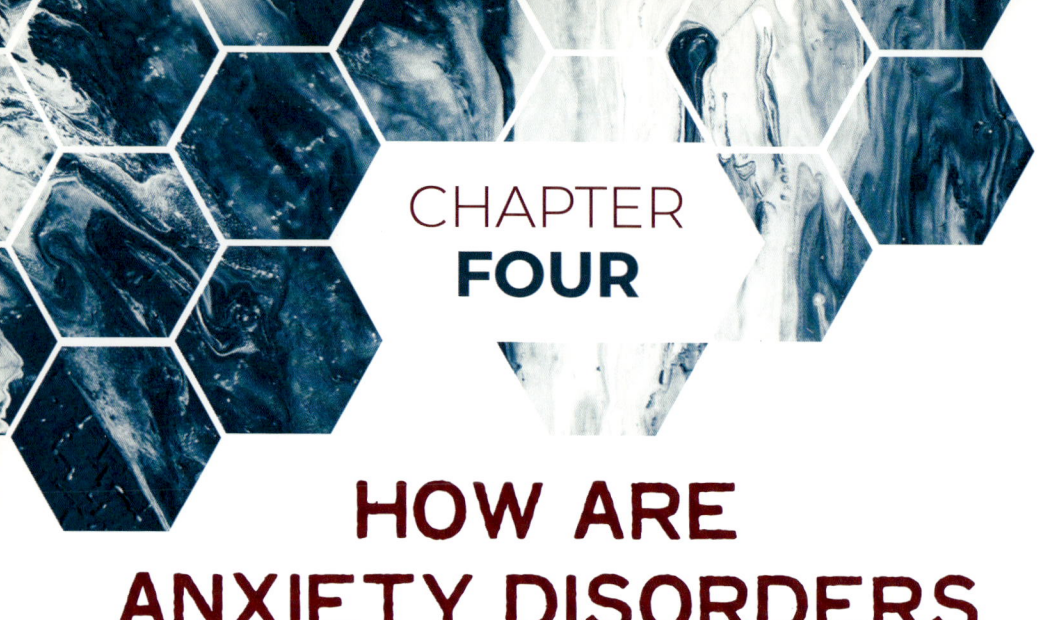

CHAPTER FOUR

HOW ARE ANXIETY DISORDERS TREATED?

There is no one-size-fits-all approach for dealing with an anxiety disorder. Each person has different experiences and requires a treatment plan that fits his or her needs. But all successful anxiety disorder treatments start the same way. In order to find treatment and relief, people with anxiety must make the crucial decision to seek help from a qualified professional. Anxiety can make it hard to reach out for help. According to the ADAA, almost two-thirds of people with anxiety disorders are untreated. Treatment for anxiety disorders can be time-consuming and expensive, but research suggests that it is worth the investment. The ADAA reports that most people who get treated for anxiety disorders are able to feel and live better. Sometimes, patients respond to treatment after just a few months.

Once a patient receives an anxiety disorder diagnosis, the work of treatment and management can begin. There are three main branches to anxiety disorder treatment. One is therapy, or treatment that involves

Only about one-third of people with anxiety seek treatment. But most people who seek treatment are able to find relief.

personal communication with a professional. Talk therapy is the most popular therapy treatment for anxiety disorders, but there are other therapies available as well. Another is medication to lessen anxiety symptoms. Finally, people with anxiety disorders may make lifestyle changes and use self-help strategies to manage their symptoms. Many times, patients will utilize a combination of these strategies simultaneously.

THERAPIES FOR ANXIETY DISORDERS

Talk therapy, also known as psychotherapy, is a popular form of anxiety disorder treatment. In talk therapy, a patient finds a trained therapist and has regular meetings with that person. The patient and therapist establish trust and privacy so that the patient can feel comfortable talking about very personal topics. Together, therapist and patient work to understand the sources of disordered anxiety, how anxiety affects the patient's life, and how to manage anxiety on a daily basis.

COGNITIVE BEHAVIORAL THERAPY

Cognitive behavioral therapy (CBT) is one of the most popular talk therapy options for anxiety disorders. CBT's name reflects its approach: the treatment method aims to change both the way patients think about their anxiety (cognition) and the way they respond to it (behavior). CBT techniques vary, but according to neuropsychologist and author Rudolph C. Hatfield, they share a goal of "changing how one perceives her own actions, the actions of the world, and her ability to affect things."[33] Patients in CBT work with therapists to identify the underlying thoughts and fears that drive their anxieties. The therapist helps show how these fears may not be realistic or useful, encouraging the patient to explore which anxieties are holding her back. Then, the patient works to adjust her worldview and feel fear and worry in realistic proportions. CBT therapists often give tasks to complete or reflection exercises to practice between sessions. For example, a patient who struggles to relax before bed might be asked to practice relaxation techniques at home every evening. Patients also learn new actions that help them manage anxiety in the moment and prepare for flare-ups of symptoms.

For example, a behavioral therapy technique called exposure therapy can help people with specific phobia disorder. In exposure therapy, patients learn to face a phobia directly and change the way they react to it. People with cynophobia, or a fear of dogs, might start introducing themselves to pictures and videos of dogs with a therapist's help. Over time, they might work to meet a dog in person. With the therapist, they can discuss how these real-life encounters were different from their fears and worries, changing their thinking about the phobia itself.

Researchers agree that CBT is an effective treatment method for anxiety disorders. David Brown was a teenager when he started suffering from severe anxiety. He had a difficult time going to school and meeting with friends, and he had some compulsive behaviors, or tics, that were out of his control. Brown began therapy with a psychologist. Brown described his experiences in therapy, saying, "He always knew kind of what to say, like talking to a close friend."[34] In his sessions, Brown learned how to identify his own triggers for anxiety and counter them with relaxation exercises. Brown felt much more able to cope with his anxiety even when he was outside his sessions. Over time, his social life and ability to succeed at school greatly improved.

> "He always knew kind of what to say, like talking to a close friend."[34]
>
> – David Brown on his therapy sessions

OTHER TALK THERAPIES

Research suggests that CBT is the most successful talk therapy approach for people with anxiety disorders. However, it is not the only type of talk therapy available. Some patients and professionals take the psychodynamic approach to therapy. Psychodynamic therapy focuses less on changing behaviors than CBT does. Instead, psychodynamic therapy looks closely at the patient's past experiences. These experiences can be from any stages of life, though the focus often may be on childhood. The therapist and patient explore how the patient's worldview was formed by the patient's early life and how negative early experiences may lead to mental health issues.

Another therapy approach is called acceptance and commitment therapy (ACT). Patients in ACT spend less time trying to understand and manage their symptoms. Instead, they work on noticing and accepting negative thoughts. The goal is to diminish the effect of symptoms of anxiety on a person's life rather than eliminate them completely. ACT patients work to separate themselves from their fearful, worrying thoughts, noticing them calmly. ACT proposes that after learning to accept their anxieties, ACT patients work to pursue their life goals with anxiety as a companion rather than an obstacle.

MARIJUANA, CBD, AND ANXIETY DISORDERS

Cannabis, in the form of marijuana, is a popular recreational and medical drug. THC is the chemical in marijuana that produces a high. For some people, smoking or ingesting marijuana can give a calm, euphoric feeling that helps counteract the symptoms of anxiety. For others, marijuana can heighten feelings of anxiety or panic. Recreational marijuana use is illegal in most parts of the United States.

Cannabidiol (CBD) is one of the main ingredients of cannabis. Unlike THC, CBD does not produce a high. CBD is often extracted from a type of cannabis plant called hemp in the form of an oil, which is legally available in most of the United States. CBD oil can be ingested directly or added to balms, sprays, or food and beverages. Advocates of CBD oil say that it can treat a variety of diseases and disorders, including anxiety. A 2015 article in the journal *Neurotherapeutics* found that moderate doses of CBD had the effect of reducing anxiety in mice and rats. However, there is no consensus on what dose of CBD is appropriate for human beings. Some CBD users report that small, regular doses of the oil help regulate anxiety. For writer Harling Ross, who has regular anxiety symptoms, "CBD relaxes me just enough to make an appreciable difference, as if I've treated my brain to a ten-minute nail salon massage."

Harling Ross, "CBD Oil Has Helped My Anxiety More Than Any Other Wellness Trend," Man Repeller, *April 25, 2018. http://manrepeller.com.*

LESS CONVENTIONAL THERAPIES

Other therapies for anxiety disorders include hypnosis or hypnotherapy, eye movement desensitization and reprocessing (EMDR), and biofeedback. In hypnotherapy, patients enter a state of deep concentration that is like a trance. Unlike in TV and movies, real-life patients in hypnotherapy always consent to be hypnotized. While the patient is in this state, the therapist suggests new feelings, ideas, and behaviors to the patient. In theory, the patient is more likely to accept these suggestions in a hypnotized state. Some patients credit hypnosis with helping them to break cycles of anxious thoughts. However, a 2016 review of research on hypnotherapy did not find evidence that the therapy was effective.

EMDR was invented by psychologist Francine Shapiro in 1987. During an EMDR session, a patient thinks about traumatic memories. At the same time, the therapist uses bilateral stimulation (such as eye movements) as part of the treatment. According to the EMDR Institute, these movements can help patients access painful memories. Then, the patient learns to associate their eye movements with new, more positive thoughts and feelings. The Institute believes that these physical movements help patients work through their feelings about difficult experiences quickly and effectively. The treatment has eight phases. As of 2019, the American Psychological Association does not specifically recommend EMDR as a treatment for anxiety disorders, although there is evidence it can help with PTSD.

Biofeedback therapy targets the physical symptoms of anxiety rather than its causes. People in biofeedback therapy are attached to machines that measure things like heart rate and body heat. Neurofeedback is a type of biofeedback therapy that measures brain waves. Patients watch

There is a variety of medications available to treat anxiety. Because different medications can affect people differently, people should only take prescribed medication as directed by a health professional.

the way their thoughts and actions change these measurements and try to control their responses. In other words, patients use feedback from the machines to manage their physical symptoms.

MEDICATIONS FOR ANXIETY DISORDERS

Clinicians prescribe many types of medications for anxiety disorders. Antidepressants and benzodiazepines are some of the most common. Each type of medication has advantages as well as drawbacks and risks.

While antidepressants were developed to treat clinical depression, they are commonly prescribed to people with anxiety disorders. Some of the most common antidepressants are selective serotonin reuptake inhibitors (SSRIs) and serotonin and norepinephrine reuptake inhibitors (SNRIs). Both of these drugs increase the brain's serotonin levels, and SNRIs also increase norepinephrine levels. These chemicals are neurotransmitters that help the brain carry signals. It's believed that low levels of these chemicals may contribute to both depression and anxiety. Popular antidepressants like Prozac and Zoloft are SSRIs. Many people who take antidepressants for anxiety find that they help relieve symptoms. However, the drugs take a few weeks to start working, and many people start to feel worse when they first start taking them. Additionally, there are side effects to their use. Common antidepressant side effects include weight gain and a lower sex drive.

Erika Vichi Lee suffered from an anxiety disorder in her teens. When she was twenty-two, a psychiatrist prescribed her Prozac. "For me, the first month on medication was straight hell," Lee wrote for *Bustle*. But after that, she started to adjust to the drug's effects on her body. After a year, she felt a new level of stability and calm. "I stopped waking up in the morning dreading my life and crying for no reason," Lee wrote.[35]

> "I stopped waking up in the morning dreading my life and crying for no reason."[35]
>
> – Erika Vichi Lee, on using antidepressants to treat an anxiety disorder

The other main group of anti-anxiety medications is benzodiazepines. This group of drugs includes Xanax, Valium, and Klonopin. Benzodiazepines work by slowing down the central nervous system. This makes them very effective in relaxing the body and mind. Unlike antidepressants, benzodiazepines begin to work quickly. They are very effective at immediately calming people in states of panic. However, benzodiazepines can be addictive. It's easy to develop a tolerance to their effects, which means users need more and more of the drug to get the same effect.

There are a few options besides antidepressants and benzodiazepines. Clinicians sometimes prescribe a medication called buspirone for GAD, but not for other anxiety disorders. Buspirone is not addictive like the benzodiazepines, but it is also not fast-acting. According to Dr. Elias Aboujaoude, who treats anxiety disorders, "buspirone can be a safer, more reasonable option" than benzodiazepines.[36] Buspirone is less popular than other anxiety medications, but prescriptions for it are on the rise. In 2017, doctors wrote 13.5 million buspirone prescriptions.

Beta-blockers work by lessening the effects of the hormone epinephrine, or adrenaline. Beta-blockers are primarily used to treat high blood pressure. They can treat some of the physical symptoms of anxiety, including dizziness, sweating, and rapid heartbeat. People might use beta-blockers to calm their nerves before a big presentation.

SELF-HELP FOR ANXIETY DISORDERS

Lifestyle changes and self-help strategies can help people with anxiety disorders manage their symptoms on a day-to-day basis. Many people find, for example, that certain foods and drinks make anxiety worse and that cutting them out helps symptoms stay under control. Experts recommend cutting down on simple carbohydrates like sweets, pastries, and pasta. These foods cause rapid blood sugar spikes, followed by lower blood sugar. Low blood sugar triggers stress hormones and can contribute to anxiety. Psychologist Margaret Wehrenberg uses the acronym CATS to remind people with anxiety disorders to beware

In addition to therapy and medication, people with anxiety can use self-help techniques to manage their symptoms. Exercise, meditation, and journaling are a few examples.

of caffeine, alcohol, tobacco, and sweeteners. All four can contribute to anxiety.

Regular exercise is an effective tool for managing anxiety. Carolyn Daitch is a clinical psychologist who treats and writes about anxiety disorders. She writes, "I have seen such startling benefits of exercise for my clients that I

> "I have seen such startling benefits of exercise for my clients that I strongly encourage all people with anxiety disorders to include exercise as part of their treatment plans."[37]
>
> – *Carolyn Daitch, therapist and anxiety expert*

strongly encourage all people with anxiety disorders to include exercise as part of their treatment plans."[37] The ADAA points out that even short, low-intensity workouts like a short walk can help relieve anxiety as well as depression. Daitch and other experts also recommend a regular sleep schedule as a useful tool to control anxiety.

People with anxiety disorders can draw from a wide array of mental and spiritual exercises to help with symptoms. Some people may find that keeping a journal helps organize their thoughts and feelings. There are worksheets and books, like the *Anxiety & Phobia Workbook*, available for anxiety disorder sufferers to organize their daily lives. Many experts recommend breathing and structured relaxation exercises as a way to control anxiety symptoms and help prevent panic attacks. For instance, by taking slow, controlled breaths, anxiety disorder sufferers can regulate the onset of anxiety symptoms. The National Health Service (NHS) of the United Kingdom describes the steps of deep breathing this way:

1. *Place one hand on your chest and the other over your stomach. You want your stomach to move more than your chest as you breathe*
2. *Take a slow, regular breath in (through your nose if you can). Watch your hands as you breathe in. The hand on your stomach should move and your chest should not*
3. *Breathe out slowly through pursed lips*
4. *Repeat this ten times, twice a day*[38]

In addition, there is evidence that mindfulness meditation can help relieve anxiety. In mindfulness meditation, the goal is to let go of conscious thoughts and feelings in order to exist in the moment. Practitioners sit in stillness and quiet, paying attention to their thoughts and emotions but also keeping a distance from them. According to meditation teacher Suzanne Westbrook, "Mindfulness teaches you the skill of paying attention to the present by noticing when your mind wanders off."[39] Research in the *JAMA Internal Medicine* review found that mindfulness meditation can lessen anxiety symptoms.

> "Mindfulness teaches you the skill of paying attention to the present by noticing when your mind wanders off."[39]
>
> – Meditation teacher Suzanne Westbrook

COMBINING APPROACHES

Dealing with an anxiety disorder can be a lifelong challenge. Symptoms may change over time or disappear only to reappear later. Sufferers of anxiety disorders work to manage their symptoms throughout life's changes and surprises. Instead of turning to a single form of treatment, many people with anxiety disorders combine approaches to manage their symptoms and live well.

In fact, many treatments for anxiety disorders work best when used in combination with other treatments. One of the main goals of CBT, for example, is to guide patients toward examining their own thoughts and decisions so they can make the best choices for their mental health. In this way, CBT can serve as an encouragement and a support for people seeking to make lifestyle changes like exercising more or cutting out anxiety-inducing substances like caffeine. Self-help strategies like exercise and guided relaxation work well to manage mild to moderate anxiety, but people who are suffering from severe symptoms may not have the ability to do them. For people who are too ill to self-regulate, medication can be an invaluable tool for lessening symptoms until they reach a more manageable level. Taking medication is not a sign of weakness. It is a tool to help anxiety sufferers get the support they need.

John Corey Whaley is a writer of young adult books. His characters struggle with anxiety disorders such as agoraphobia and must navigate relationships with friends and family who do not share their disorders. Whaley draws on his own experiences with anxiety disorders in his writing. He uses several approaches to manage his anxiety. "I've found that a combination of therapy and

> "I've found that a combination of therapy and medication, along with lifestyle choices like eating better and exercising regularly, helps me cope well with my anxiety."[40]
> – John Corey Whaley, YA writer

FAAH-OUT MUTATIONS AND ANXIETY

Anxiety is part of the human condition. However, just as there are people who experience severe levels of anxiety, there are some people who rarely feel anxious. Some even feel no anxiety at all. Jo Cameron is one extreme example. The Scottish woman cannot feel pain. Throughout her life, she has not felt fear or anxiety about any situation in life. Sometimes she injures herself and does not even notice that she's been hurt. She also doesn't feel anxiety in dangerous situations and has never felt an adrenaline rush. Cameron has never taken pain medication, even after major surgeries. When she didn't need painkillers after surgery at sixty-five years old, her doctor sent her to a pain geneticist.

Doctors discovered that Cameron has a rare genetic mutation. She is missing part of a gene called FAAH-OUT. Scientists believe that this mutation is responsible for Cameron's lack of pain. They also think that Cameron's inability to feel pain and her very low levels of anxiety are related. In addition, Cameron is a very forgetful person. Her memory problems may also be linked to her painlessness and lack of anxiety. Researchers are studying Cameron's gene mutations in order to better understand the genetic basis of anxiety and pain. They are curious about whether the mutation can point the way to new treatments for pain and anxiety disorders.

medication, along with lifestyle choices like eating better and exercising regularly, helps me cope well with my anxiety," Whaley told *BuzzFeed*.[40]

BREAKING THE STIGMA AND RAISING AWARENESS

Even though anxiety disorders are common, people who suffer from anxiety can feel alone in their struggles. In US society, people with mental illnesses face stigma, or widespread negative judgment. Some people believe that mental disorders are not as real as physical illnesses, or that people with mental disorders like anxiety are just complaining too much about everyday thoughts and feelings. This stigma can make people with anxiety disorders feel that they are weak or wrong for talking about their disorder or seeking the support of others. They may get the message that they should be able to cope with anxiety on their own. Negative cultural messages about people with mental illnesses can worsen the feelings of shame and isolation that people with anxiety disorders struggle with.

By speaking out about their experiences with anxiety disorders, some people hope to show others that they are not alone. Some people have found freedom by sharing their struggles with mental disorders with friends and family. Aparna Nancherla is a comedian who struggles with depression and anxiety disorder. She's benefited from the decision to share her experiences with loved ones. "Multiple members of my family deal with depression and anxiety so it's become a more open conversation now, which is really great and important, and has only brought us closer," Nancherla says.[41] Nancherla discusses her mental disorders in her work, sharing her experiences with audiences through comedy. Similarly, Whaley feels that talking about his mental disorder is freeing. "I've also found that writing about my experience with mental

Many people and organizations work to educate people about anxiety disorders. Through education, they can help people seek treatment.

illness has really helped me understand myself and my illness better and that has done wonders for my health," Whaley told *BuzzFeed*.[42]

There are nonprofit organizations devoted to supporting people with mental disorders through information, resources, and advocacy. NAMI began in 1979. The organization describes itself as "the nation's largest grassroots mental health organization dedicated to building better lives for the millions of Americans affected by mental illness."[43] NAMI offers a helpline for people with mental disorders who are struggling to find treatment or need immediate support. Much of NAMI's work centers around policy advocacy and awareness. The organization's policy wing works to direct more funding and research to the treatment of mental disorders, and it pushes for expanded insurance coverage for people with mental illnesses and disorders. NAMI also organizes NAMIWalks, 3.1-mile (5-km) walks where participants gather together to show their support for people with mental disorders and raise money for the organization.

The ADAA was also founded in 1979. It focuses on providing information and treatment resources for people with anxiety disorders, depression, and related disorders like OCD and PTSD. The ADAA publicizes new research and treatment methods for anxiety disorders and encourages mental health providers to learn about them. It also maintains a directory of mental health providers across the United States who are qualified to treat anxiety disorders.

In the United States, advocates and lawmakers are working to educate more young people about mental disorders. In 2018, the states of New York and Virginia passed laws requiring public schools to add mental health education to their curricula. Supporters of these laws hope that teaching students to recognize and understand the symptoms of mental disorders will help more people find early treatment and support. "Mental health treatment is much more effective if the disease is caught early," Dustin Verga, a high school teacher and supporter of the law, told journalists.[44]

In a way, educating the next generation about how to recognize and fight anxiety disorders can be a form of public psychoeducation. By learning how anxiety disorders work, how to diagnose them, and how to treat them, more people can find the resources and support to live lives that aren't held back by fear.

SOURCE NOTES

INTRODUCTION: WHEN WORRY TAKES OVER

1. Quoted in "Impact of the DSM-IV to DSM-5 Changes on the National Survey on Drug Use and Health [Internet]," *NCBI*, June 2016. http://ncbi.nlm.nih.gov.
2. "Understand the Facts: Generalized Anxiety Disorder (GAD)," *Anxiety and Depression Association of America*, n.d. http://adaa.org.
3. "Understanding Anxiety Disorders: When Panic, Fear, and Worries Overwhelm," *News in Health (NIH)*, March 2016. http://newsinhealth.nih.gov.
4. Quoted in "Understanding Anxiety Disorders," *NIH*.
5. Quoted in "Understanding Anxiety Disorders," *NIH*.

CHAPTER 1: WHAT ARE ANXIETY DISORDERS?

6. Quoted in Jenna Birch, "This Is the Difference Between Normal Anxiety and an Anxiety Disorder," *HuffPost*, May 14, 2019. http://huffpost.com.
7. *Diagnostic and Statistical Manual of Mental Disorders (DSM-5)*. Washington, DC: American Psychiatric Association Publishing, 2013, p. 20.
8. Jessica, "Living with Emetophobia," *Time to Change*, April 5, 2013. http://time-to-change.org.uk.
9. *DSM-5*, p. 203.
10. Quoted in Korin Miller, "6 Things People Need to Stop Getting Wrong About Social Anxiety," *Self.com*, April 12, 2018. http://self.com.
11. Quinn, "Quinn's Story—Generalised Anxiety Disorder," *Understanding Anxiety*, n.d. http://wayahead.org.au.
12. Kelly Jensen and Lisa Jakub, *(Don't) Call Me Crazy: 33 Voices Start the Conversation About Mental Health*. Chapel Hill: Algonquin Books, 2018, p. 152.
13. @SaraJBenincasa, *Twitter*, 10 Oct. 2018, 1:12 p.m., twitter.com/SaraJBenincasa/status/1050116874216853509.
14. Quoted in Ashley Mateo, "This Is What It's Like to Be an Adult with Separation Anxiety," *Health.com*, November 19, 2018. http://health.com.
15. Quoted in Rebecca Kamm, "What It's Like to Have a Phobia of Talking," *Vice*, January 23, 2017. http://vice.com.

CHAPTER 2: HOW ARE ANXIETY DISORDERS DIAGNOSED?

16. Allan V. Horwitz, *Anxiety: A Short History*. Baltimore: Johns Hopkins University Press, 2013, p. 98.

17. Horwitz, *Anxiety*, p. 128.

18. Carolyn Daitch, *Anxiety Disorders: The Go-To Guide for Clients and Therapists*. New York: W.W. Norton, 2011, p. 19.

19. "Adding Better Mental Health Care to Primary Care," *National Institute of Mental Health*, December 30, 2016. http://nimh.nih.gov.

20. *DSM-5*, p. 225.

21. Quoted in Daitch, *Anxiety Disorders*, p. 34.

22. Tracy Clayton, "When Taking Anxiety Medication Is a Revolutionary Act," *BuzzFeed News*, February 11, 2015. http://buzzfeednews.com.

23. Quoted in Sarah Schuster, "32 People Describe What It's Like Living with Both Anxiety and Depression," *The Mighty*, November 1, 2016. http://themighty.com.

24. Rebecca J. Stokes, "What It Feels Like to Have Anxiety and Depression at the Same Time," *YourTango*, June 14, 2018. http://yourtango.com.

CHAPTER 3: WHAT IS LIFE LIKE WITH ANXIETY DISORDERS?

25. Caryn Blanton, "Coping with COPD and Anxiety," *American Lung Association*, November 27, 2018. http://lung.org.

26. Una McCann, "Anxiety and Heart Disease," *Johns Hopkins Medicine*, n.d. http://hopkinsmedicine.org.

27. Paul Mite, "Social Anxiety: Paul—Part 1," *Social Anxiety Institute*, May 28, 2013. www.youtube.com.

28. Justin Bayshore, "How You See Yourself & the World," *Social Anxiety Institute*, September 29, 2016. www.youtube.com.

29. Laura Bartley, "This Is What It's Like to Live with Agoraphobia," *Metro*, October 26, 2017. http://metro.co.uk.

30. Quoted in Kamm, "What It's Like to Have a Phobia of Talking."

31. Reddit user 001635468798, "Mini Rant: Tokophobia: Comments," *Reddit*, May 11, 2018. http://reddit.com.

32. Quoted in Lindsay Holmes, "16 Things People with Social Anxiety Want You to Know," *HuffPost*, July 13, 2015. http://huffpost.com.

SOURCE NOTES CONTINUED

CHAPTER 4: HOW ARE ANXIETY DISORDERS TREATED?

33. Rudolph C. Hatfield, *The Everything Guide to Coping with Panic Disorder: Learn How to Take Control of Your Panic and Live a Healthier, Happier Life*. Avon: Simon & Schuster, 2013, p. 155.

34. Quoted in "A Teenager Learns How to Overcome Anxiety," *Yale Medicine*, February 28, 2017. http://yalemedicine.org.

35. Erika V. Lee, "Why It Took So Long for My Asian American Parents to Accept My Decision to Take Antidepressants," *Bustle*, May 8, 2018. http://bustle.com.

36. Quoted in Roni Rabin, "Shortage of Anxiety Drug Leaves Patients Scrambling," *The New York Times*, February 1, 2019. http://nytimes.com.

37. Daitch, *Anxiety Disorders*, p. 198.

38. "Relaxation Techniques," *NHS Inform,* n.d. http://nhsinform.scot.

39. Quoted in Liz Mineo, "With Mindfulness, Life's in the Moment," *The Harvard Gazette,* April 17, 2018. http://news.harvard.edu.

40. Quoted in Krystie L. Yandoli, "How One Author Is Motivated by His Chronic Anxiety," *BuzzFeed*, December 10, 2015. http://buzzfeed.com.

41. Quoted in Lindsay Holmes and Catharine Smith, "Aparna Nancherla Is Depressed, Sad, Overwhelmed—and Laughing," *HuffPost*, July 13, 2018. http://huffpost.com.

42. Quoted in "How One Author Is Motivated by His Chronic Anxiety."

43. "About NAMI," *NAMI*, n.d. http://nami.org.

44. Quoted in Christine Vestal, "States Begin Requiring Mental Health Education in Schools," *NAMI Virginia*, June 23, 2018. http://namivirginia.org.

FOR FURTHER RESEARCH

BOOKS

American Psychiatric Association, *Diagnostic and Statistical Manual of Mental Disorders*. Washington, DC: American Psychiatric Publishing, 2013.

David A. Clark et al., *The Anxiety & Worry Workbook: The Cognitive Behavioral Solution*. New York: Guilford Press, 2011.

Carol Hand, *Living with Anxiety Disorders*. Minneapolis, MN: Abdo Publishing, 2014.

Rudolph C. Hatfield, *The Everything Guide to Coping with Panic Disorder*. New York: Everything, 2014.

Kelly Jensen, *(Don't) Call Me Crazy: 33 Voices Start the Conversation About Mental Health*. New York: Algonquin Young Readers, 2018.

Carla Mooney, *What Is Anxiety Disorder?* San Diego, CA: ReferencePoint Press, 2016.

INTERNET SOURCES

"Anxiety and Physical Illness," *Harvard Health Publishing*, May 9, 2018. www.health.harvard.edu.

Caroline Beaton, "Is Anxiety a White-People Thing?" *Vice*, November 9, 2017. www.vice.com.

"Panic Attack Symptoms," *Web MD*, 2017. www.webmd.com.

Brittany Risher, "This Is When to See a Mental Health Professional About Your Anxiety," *SELF Magazine*, February 2, 2018. www.self.com.

WEBSITES

Anxiety and Depression Association of America (ADAA)
https://adaa.org

The ADAA offers information and support for people who suffer from anxiety and/or depression.

Headspace
https://headspace.org.au

Headspace is an Australian mental health organization that provides resources, education, and mental health support to people ages 12–25.

National Association of Mental Illness (NAMI)
www.nami.org

NAMI conducts research and advocacy on behalf of people with mental illness. It also offers resources like a mental health helpline.

INDEX

Aboujaoude, Elias, 62
Adele, 17
alcohol, 47, 63
Alvarez, Jackie, 52
American Psychological Association (APA), 26–27, 31
Anxiety and Depression Association of America (ADAA), 8, 32–33, 39, 47, 54, 64, 69
Anxiety & Phobia Workbook, 64
anxiety disorders in animals, 29
athletes, 17
autism, 41

Bartley, Laura, 49, 50, 51
Bayshore, Justin, 48
behavioral psychology, 28–30
Benincasa, Sara, 21
Birndorf, Catherine, 51
Blanton, Caryn, 46
Brown, David, 57
Bustle, 61
BuzzFeed, 67–68

caffeine, 23, 62–63, 65
Cameron, Jo, 66
cannabidiol (CBD), 58
Carmin, Cheryl, 12
Center for Workplace Mental Health, 52
childhood, 14, 18, 21, 22, 28, 41, 57
childhood trauma, 41
chronic obstructive pulmonary disease (COPD), 45–46
Clark, Anna, 22, 50

Clayton, Tracy, 37–38
clinical depression, 41–43, 60
cynophobia, 56

Daitch, Carolyn, 31, 37, 63–64
Depression and Anxiety, 52
diagnosing anxiety disorders, 12, 14, 19, 21, 23–24, 26–27, 33, 34–35, 36, 37, 38–40, 43, 54
Diagnostic and Statistical Manual of Mental Disorders, 5th Edition (DSM-5), 13, 14, 16, 20, 24, 26–27, 28, 34, 36, 37, 40
doctors, 7, 24, 28, 30–31, 33–34, 62, 66

education, 69
EMDR Institute, 59
exercise, 56–57, 63–64, 65

Forti, Allison, 22
Freud, Sigmund, 28

Grant, Hugh, 17

Hatfield, Rudolph C., 56
high school, 4, 69
Horwitz, Allan, 28

Immunology and Allergy Clinics of North America, 46
irritable bowel syndrome (IBS), 44–45

Jakub, Lisa, 19
JAMA Internal Medicine, 65

Lee, Erika Vichi, 61

marijuana, 58
McCann, Una, 46

Mental Health America, 32–33
Mite, Paul, 47–48
musicians, 17

Nancherla, Aparna, 67
National Alliance on Mental Illness (NAMI), 32, 68–69
National Health Service (NHS) of the United Kingdom, 64
National Institutes of Health (NIH), 8
Neurotherapeutics, 58
New York, 69
nonprofit organizations, 68

obsessive-compulsive disorder (OCD), 24, 69
optimal anxiety, 12

panic attacks, 17, 18–20, 21, 24, 40, 49–50, 51, 64
parts of the brain
    amygdala, 25
    hippocampus, 25
Pavlov, Ivan, 29–30
Pine, Daniel, 8–9
post-traumatic stress disorder (PTSD), 24, 59, 69
postpartum anxiety (PPA), 51
pregnancy, 50, 51
psychiatrists, 8, 27, 28, 33, 34–35, 36, 46, 51, 61
psychoanalysis, 28
psychoeducation, 37, 69
psychologists, 12, 27, 28–30, 31, 33, 37, 56–57, 59, 62–63

relationships, 8–9, 12, 44, 47, 52–53, 66
Ross, Harling, 58

Shapiro, Francine, 59
sleep, 7, 10–11, 18, 34–35, 36, 41–43, 44, 51, 64
Social Anxiety Institute, 48
social workers, 33, 46
stigmas, 67
Stokes, Rebecca Jane, 43
Streisand, Barbra, 17
symptoms of anxiety
    chest pain, 18
    compulsive behaviors, 24, 57
    depersonalization, 19
    derealization, 19
    difficulty concentrating, 4, 8, 11, 34–35, 52
    dizziness, 18, 40, 44, 62
    fast breathing, 10, 16, 18, 23, 46
    fears, 4, 8–9, 10, 12, 14, 16, 18, 20–21, 30, 40, 46, 50, 56–57
    feeling cold, 11, 18
    feeling overheated, 11, 18
    feeling tense, 5, 10–12, 16, 34, 40, 44
    headaches, 7, 40, 44
    nausea, 18, 47
    paresthesia, 18
    racing heart, 16, 18–19, 46, 47, 62
    repetitive thoughts, 11, 21, 24
    shaking, 10, 18

INDEX CONTINUED

stress, 7, 8, 12, 17, 21, 24, 30, 39, 41–42, 45–46, 47, 62
sweating, 10, 16, 18, 62
tiredness, 7, 16, 34–35
upset stomach, 10, 18, 44–45
worries, 4–7, 8, 10, 12, 14, 16, 18, 22, 23, 36–37, 40, 47, 50–51, 52, 56–57, 58

therapies for anxiety disorders
  acceptance and commitment therapy (ACT), 58
  antidepressant medications, 60–62
  benzodiazepines, 60–62
  biofeedback therapy, 59
  cognitive behavioral therapy (CBT), 56–57, 65
  exposure therapy, 56
  eye movement desensitization and reprocessing (EMDR), 59
  hypnotherapy, 59
  psychodynamic therapy, 57
  self-help strategies, 9, 32–33, 55, 62, 65–66

tobacco, 46–47, 62–63
tokophobia, 50, 51
Twitter, 16
types of anxiety disorders
  agoraphobia, 14, 20–21, 49, 50, 66
  generalized anxiety disorder, 7–8, 14, 16–18, 34–35, 36, 37, 40, 51, 62
  other specified anxiety disorder, 14, 23–24
  panic disorder, 14, 18–20, 51

selective mutism, 14, 22, 50
separation anxiety disorder, 14, 21–22, 29
social anxiety disorder, 14, 16, 17, 36–37, 47–48
specific phobias, 14–15, 50, 56
substance/medication-induced anxiety disorder, 14, 23
unspecified anxiety disorder, 14, 23

Verga, Dustin, 69
Vice, 50
Virginia, 69

Wehrenberg, Margaret, 62–63
Westbrook, Suzanne, 65
Whaley, John Corey, 66–67, 68
World Health Organization (WHO), 40, 52
World War II, 28–29

IMAGE CREDITS

Cover: © Antonio Guillem/Shutterstock Images
5: © Star Stock/Shutterstock Images
6: © Star Stock/Shutterstock Images
9: © Atstock Productions/Shutterstock Images
11: © Antonio Guillem/Shutterstock Images
15: © maxim ibragimov/Shutterstock Images
20: © Pepgooner/Shutterstock Images
25: © Blamb/Shutterstock Images
27: © New Africa/Shutterstock Images
32: © Monkey Business Images/Shutterstock Images
35: © StasyKID/Shutterstock Images
38: © Pormezz/Shutterstock Images
42: © Monkey Business Images/Shutterstock Images
45: © fizkes/Shutterstock Images
49: © Motortion Films/Shutterstock Images
53: © Antonio Guillem/Shutterstock Images
55: © Photographee.eu/Shutterstock Images
60: © Dmytro Zinkevych/Shutterstock Images
63: © Alena Ozerova/Shutterstock Images
68: © Photographee.eu/Shutterstock Images

ABOUT THE AUTHOR

A.W. Buckey is a writer and pet-sitter living in Brooklyn, New York.